I MADE IT OUT

With A Sound Mind

CHERYL EDWARDS

I MADE IT OUT
With A Sound Mind

Copyright © 2023 Cheryl Edwards

All rights reserved. Printed in the United States of America. No part of this book may be used or reproduced in any manner whatsoever without written permission except in the case of brief quotations in critical articles or reviews.

Typesetting, Book Layout, Editing and Cover Design by
Enger Lanier Taylor for In Due Season Publishing

Published By: In Due Season Publishing ®
Huntsville, Alabama
indueseasonpublishing@gmail.com

ISBN-13: 978-1-970057-42-3
ISBN-10: 1-970057-42-4

Cheryl Edwards

TABLE OF CONTENTS

DEDICATION 5

INTRODUCTION 7
   DRUGGING TO LIVE & LIVING TO DRUG

CHAPTER ONE 9
   WHAT A MESS

CHAPTER TWO 15
   PARTY OVER HERE

CHAPTER THREE 21
   THIS WAS ONLY A TRAP

CHAPTER FOUR 28
   I COULDN'T RUN AWAY FROM ME

CHAPTER FIVE 36
   THE SINKHOLE

CHAPTER SIX 53
   THE TURNAROUND

CHAPTER SEVEN 69
   I AM A MIRACLE, SIGN & AND A WONDER

SCRIPTURES & CONFESSIONS 72

BIOGRAPHY 76

YOUTUBE INTERVIEW QR CODE 77

Cheryl Edwards

Dedication

I give all Glory, Honor, and praise to my Lord and Savior, Jesus Christ. Despite all my imperfections, He gave His life for me, and He kept me. I will forever glorify, magnify, and exalt Him. Thank you, Jesus, for all you have done and continue to do in my life.

I dedicate this book to my children, Ryan and Dorion, for loving me despite not understanding what was happening with me. Especially my daughter Ryan because I know it was hard for you, but you did your best to love me through this long, drawn-out journey and found it in your heart to truly forgive me and cheer me on. I am incredibly grateful for you, Dorion, because no matter what, I have always been the best mama in your eyes. I love you both with everything I have.

To my mom, Walterene, you are the epitome of a mother's love. You did your best to love me through my addiction and never left me. I will be forever grateful for everything you have done and continue to do for me. You took care of my children so they would not end up in the system, and for that alone, I'm grateful. Words could never express how much that means to me. I love you, mama.

Cheryl Edwards

Introduction

Drugging to Live and Living to Drug

I made it out with a sound mind!! The way I describe my drug and alcohol addiction is going from a *pothole* to a *ditch* to a *sinkhole* and then to a *manhole*. The progression of my addiction was real, and it began to feel like I was at a point of no return. In my lowest moments, I knew God had a hedge around me, and I would confess that to the other addicts, I was around because the feeling was so real. People were dying with the crack pipe in their hands, and I knew the way I smoked, and as much as I smoked, for as long as I smoked, and the way I lived, there was no way I should still be standing. BUT GOD…

I know all too well what being caught up in the grip of drug and alcohol addiction is like, living to drug and drugging to live. I thank God for His Word because it is so true, "Who the Son set free is free indeed" (John 8:36). All the glory, honor, and praise belongs to my Lord and Savior Jesus Christ because He came to set the captive (me) free. It was His Word through a willing vessel that pricked my heart and had me concerned about my soul (Psalms

107:20). He sent His Word, and it healed them and delivered them from their destruction, yes, by the power of His Word. I was set free. I often say He left the ninety-nine to come get me. This is my story but God's glory, and I want you to know no matter how long you have been bound and what the bondage is, God is still in the delivering business.

Chapter 1

What A Mess – The Early Years

While in my addiction to crack cocaine, marijuana, alcohol, and the lifestyle that goes with it, I knew there was going to come a time that I would be set free. I also knew that I was in too deep to walk away from doing drugs and alcohol no matter how badly I wanted to. God had to do it because I tried, and I could not. I could stop, but I could not quit! I call that a *pause*. The few times I could stop were because I had no money, people didn't need me to run and get drugs for them, or I was just exhausted to the point that I would pass out and sleep for a few days. But once I was rested, I was back up and off to the races. I prayed for it to STOP! I would say to myself and out loud from time to time, "God, why don't you just let me have a nervous breakdown or let a doctor tell me if I take one more puff, I was going to die"? (how would a doctor tell me that because you are bound in drug and alcohol addiction and the last place you go is to the doctor even if you need to?). God knew I really didn't desire either; I just wanted to be free. For a while, I really didn't think I had a problem. For a long time, the only problem I had was individuals telling me I had a problem, especially those who were just as addicted to drugs and alcohol as I was. They had no problem telling me I needed help but couldn't see how messed up they were, and they needed help as well.

I was a full-blown crackhead for 32 years of my life. Until the last eight years of my addiction, I was a functional addict. Everything I did was done under the influence. If that wasn't deception, I don't know what it was. I lost many jobs, fired myself off jobs, sabotaged many relationships, and hurt almost everyone who would get too close to me. Later in my deliverance process, it was proven that drugs were just the manifestation of what was really going on with me. I was harboring a deep, dark secret that I never uttered to anyone. I can still hear those words, "You better not tell anyone because no one will believe you anyway." Those words muted and paralyzed me, making it hard to tell anyone. I felt as though no one would believe me. I kept that deep, dark secret to myself for most of my life, and it haunted me.

THE DEVASTATION OF DIVORCE...

I really hate to admit that I come from a traumatized environment. I thought my family's dysfunctional behavior was normal: parents fighting, arguing, yelling, and cursing constantly. My parents divorced when I was in the 2nd grade, and from my perspective, my mom woke up one day, sat my three siblings and me on the bed, and told us that the marriage between her and my father was not going to work and the next thing I knew we were packed up and moving out. I was crushed, my world had been shattered and torn into pieces because I was a daddy's girl, and now we were moving to a new place without him. Moving into our new home, the fighting and arguing did not stop. For a while, there was chaos over child support.

My mom eventually said forget it, and I remember her working two or three jobs to care for her babies and maintain a roof over our heads. I remember crying and praying they would get along so the arguing would stop. They eventually came to a neutral place where they could communicate and decided to split the children up. But the two girls must stay together, and the same with the two boys; the choice was the children's. (That decision should have never been given to children because we were too young). Divorce is devastating for the children. In my opinion, it affects every aspect of children's lives. This was the beginning of me being allowed to make choices I was not mature enough to make. I chose to live with my dad not only because I was a daddy's girl but because that's where the rules were not so strict (except when it came to my stepmom). See, that's where all the fun party people were. Everyone on my mom's side of the family was educated and very rigid. I don't remember spending much time with them until I got a little older, although they visited occasionally.

By the age of nine, which was 4th grade, both of my parents had remarried. My stepmom was saved and went to church most of the time, and for whatever reason, she wasn't very nice. She would make us go to church all the time. I always felt that was because her children were grown, and now her husband was brought up in a different environment with four young children who were not her own. She didn't allow us to do many things other children could do, such as go to the movies and listen to music other than gospel. We could not watch television unless it was what she was watching: soap operas or church shows. There was no fingernail polish, no talking on the phone; she would keep the phone in our reach unplugged, no talking to boys, and definitely no spending the night over at anyone's house, even if they were family. However, she ensured we were very well dressed in the best clothing and shoes. The house's decor was beautiful, and she would make us go to church all day every Sunday. We didn't understand why she was so strict, especially because it was said (through the grapevine) that she was the reason my parents split up.

    We would visit my mom on the weekends. My mom was a hard worker and focused on providing for her children while trying to maintain her peace. She owned her own hair salon and worked multiple jobs outside the home, so we spent a lot of time with my stepfather. There were times when she worked in the salon for countless hours, and after she closed the shop, she would report to a different job at night, so there were many nights she wasn't home. My stepfather was then left with us, and he was seemingly a very nice guy when it came to us. He never mistreated us regarding verbal abuse, but there were other issues. He would creep around the house in the middle of the night. I would hear him sneaking around, and it never failed; he would end up in my bedroom, fondling me. This continued from 4th grade up until my freshman year of high school. I would lay there and play possum. He thought

I was in a deep sleep. I hated it. I would lay there terrified, not asleep at all, just too afraid to move, wanting to scream but couldn't. However, this didn't just happen in the middle of the night; there were times I would be outside playing and run in the house for a glass of water or a snack, and he would corner me and make me lay across his lap and stick his hands in my clothes. This would make me cringe. I remember my friends would ask me what was wrong because my attitude would change when I came back outside. He was very quick about it, and he would tell me, "You better not tell anybody. This is our secret, and they won't believe you anyway." By my freshman year, enough was enough, and I was determined that I was not staying in that house another night as long as he was there.

YOU ARE ONLY AS DARK AS YOUR SECRETS...

This deep, dark secret of being physically violated took me to some places within myself that I could not explain. It affected every aspect of my life. I felt so dirty, ashamed, and all alone because I couldn't understand why this was happening for the life of me. I attempted many times to tell someone, but I would hear him whispering, "You better not tell anybody. This is our little secret; if you tell, nobody will believe you anyway." I honestly thought that no one would believe me. I was always told I was too grown and disrespectful when, in reality, I was not. I was hurting and did not know how to convey that I was being violated to anyone because, in the back of my mind, I felt it was my fault.

My mom and my stepfather eventually ended up

divorcing after numerous fights and arguments, which led to scuffles from time to time. My mom was still unaware of what had been happening to me. So, as a child, throughout my young adolescent years and into my adulthood, I kept this deep, dark secret to myself. There was not one person I felt I could tell this story who I thought would believe me. I had cousins that were more like my sisters, that I shared everything, but I could not bring myself to tell them this was happening to me.

Chapter 2

Party Over Here
Where It All Started

While in middle school through my freshman year of high school, I would visit my mom's house on the weekends, and when I returned to my father's house on Sundays, where the family and friends would have Sunday dinners together. Each family would bring a dish and a bottle. They would play cards, play music, dance, laughed, and just have a good time. This is really where I believe the addiction began. I think this is the place that I would call the *pothole* because it was fun and would help me mask the pain. I had an aunt who was not much older than us, was married, and owned a home on the next block. Once we ate dinner, the dishes were completed, and the adults were in their groove, the teenagers would ease out and go over to their house and party, which consisted of smoking marijuana and drinking. We thought that was cool because they would lay down the law that we better not ever be caught drinking and smoking marijuana with anyone outside the family. So now all the teenagers looked forward to Sundays so we could go over to my aunt and uncle's house because it was going down. For me, Sunday gatherings were where I could forget about the pain I had endured the weekend, thinking this was a way of escape, only to find out later in life that being high only magnified the problem because once I would come down off the high, the problem was still there.

While I was growing up, alcohol was always around. I hate to say it, but my father worked 16 hours a day for as long as I knew him, and I remember him having a drink every day. He had a refrigerator in the basement and one in the garage that was always stocked with beer, although I never saw him drunk. To be honest, I don't have many memories of high school other than I would have a 16o.z. can of beer (Old English 800 or Schlitz Malt Liquor Bull) and a joint every morning before 1st period during my senior year. I don't remember anything about my senior year of high school except that I slept through history, which was my first class. I don't know how I passed that class, but I did. Although I thought this was fun, it was the beginning of my spiral into the grip of addiction.

By the time I reached high school in 1976, I was already much more advanced than my peers. Every guy I dated was a pothead (the slang name for people who smoked marijuana all the time), and they drank beer or liquor. In my last year of high school, I joined a modeling troop. We called ourselves "A Touch Of Class." I started modeling in the local nightclub Ebony Terrace Lounge. I was definitely too young to be allowed in, so they would let me model and send me home right after the show; they would not let me hang around.

My dad worked midnights, and he would leave the house at 10:30 p.m. and by 10:35 p.m. I would be sneaking out the door. My grandmother lived next door, and she would see me sneak out of the house almost every night after my father left. She would threaten to tell on me, but she never did. One thing she would do is sit in her big picture window with the curtains drawn until she saw me come up the driveway, and I would see her hand wave through the curtain. That was her way of letting me know she saw me sneak out and back in. We would go to her house every morning to watch for the bus because we could see the corner from her window, and she would let me know she saw me and would tell me when I left and when I came back. She hated for us to get in trouble, so she kept that a secret and took it to her grave. I look back now and wonder if my life would've turned out differently if she had told on me. I'm sure it would've because my parents didn't play. I am certainly not blaming my grandmother for my actions. However, I am sure there may have been a different outcome if I had suffered the consequences earlier. But I have since decided that God knew every step I would make before He rescued me and that it was all a part of the big picture. How else could I convince others of what He could do unless he had done it in and for me?

MOVING TOO FAST

From modeling in the club, I became acquainted with a gentleman five years older than me. This is where my addiction took a turn and went to a whole different level, which I call the *ditch,* because I entered his world where I was introduced to sniffing cocaine. I thought this was still fun because I was not only dating an older guy, but he was fine, and to me, my peers were lame and square. After graduating from high school six months early because

I had all my credits, I decided to move out and live with my boyfriend. He had a good job, and he took good care of me. I thought I was grown and no longer wanted to follow any rules at home. I wanted to come and go as I pleased and didn't want anyone telling me what I could and could not do. In the beginning, it was fun. He went to work, I went to cosmetology school, I did hair on the side in my mom's beauty salon, and after work, we would go out and play pool at this bar called Ruby's 711. This is where everybody would hang out, and after the club would close, everybody would go to the after-set, usually at someone's house. This is where a select few were allowed to go and gamble, drink, and get high. Lord knows I was too young to be in the company of these grown folks, but I was all up in it. We would hang out until the wee hours of the night. Eventually, it got to a point where he didn't want me to hang out because his ex-girlfriend would show up, and he never wanted us in the same place at the same time, and when we were, he would enjoy making me think it was still something going on with them. This became a problem in our home because there were times he wouldn't come home, and being young and dumb and not knowing how to deal with that would cause us to constantly argue (I was the instigator of the arguments), and he would use that as an excuse to stay out for days.

    Fussing and arguing became a part of our household, like when I was a child. Thinking he was with another woman caused me to start snooping around, only to find out that the other woman was a crack pipe and he was hanging out in places where freebasing (smoking cocaine, which they cooked into rock form themselves) was ok.

I MADE IT OUT

During this time, I was sniffing cocaine a little bit, and freebasing was a NO..NO. Finally, the disappearing acts became too much, and he got tired of me snooping around and popping up, blowing his high, so he started allowing me to go with him. Once I started hanging out with him a little too often, he decided he didn't want me in that atmosphere, so we came to an agreement that he could smoke at home (because it was no longer a secret), only to find out now I would be the one he smoked with. It didn't take long before we verbally vowed that I would not be smoking with anyone but him. Eventually, smoking marijuana became secondary, although drinking was my norm. People drank water, and Cheryl drank beer.

If you know anything about drugs, it's definitely not something that a couple can do together because it opens the door to chaos, confusion, and no peace—constantly fighting and arguing about who is going to get the most, both of you paranoid and constantly arguing if not fighting. Well, that is exactly what started happening, and it caused him to start finding other places to get high where he couldn't be found because all we would do was argue and fight. This went on for approximately 6-7 years, then eventually, he broke up with me and started dating someone who didn't do drugs or drink at all. She didn't even smoke cigarettes. My verbal vow became my nightmare. Not only did he leave me for her, but he left me with a habit for a sober woman, or so I thought. Many years later, I learned she did drugs as well.

I was crushed! I moved out and went to live with my cousin, I would lay in bed for weeks crying. At that time, I had just started a new job traveling with a black skin regimen. My job was to launch a product in the JC Penney stores on the East Coast. Thank God for my boss at the time because one day he had had enough because now this was affecting the business. I would call in and tell him I was sick too many times, which was very unusual. One day, out of the blue, he said to me, "You have been sick and crying for two weeks. You must be having man problems, and believe me, you will not die. I can only see you crying this long because you don't think you are desirable to anyone else." Cheryl, do you think you are desirable to anyone else? I had to really stop and think about that question because I did not know how to answer that because I didn't even know if I desired myself, who I was, or know my worth. This dude was gone on about his life, and the only thing I was stuck with was a habit. Now that I look back, I think that was the issue because he was my supplier. I got up, shook myself, fixed myself up, and started traveling again for about two months.

Chapter 3

This Was Only A Trap

I moved to Bolingbrook with my mom, who had sold her house, and moved in with a friend who also allowed me to stay there. My mom had some really good friends. A husband and wife who worked for her had introduced her to a nice guy, a kingpin drug dealer, and my mom didn't know it, but I did! He was really nice to her and he was really nice to me. I knew him through my ex, and when he found out that I was my mom's child he had compassion for what I was going through. I happened to be at his house one day with my mom's friend who worked with her but was my age, and I was arguing with my ex on the phone. After I got off the phone, I was crying. He sat me down and asked me, "Why are you crying?" I shared with him what had happened between us that caused us to break up and how it was tough to stay away from him because I loved him, and he provided for me. I went on to share that he would give me money, although we were no longer dating. I didn't want to tell the truth that he was still giving me drugs and getting me high when we would get together.

He gave me a proposition, he asked me if I truly wanted to get away from him. I responded yes, so he started to give me money occasionally, then offered me a job. He would send me down the street to FedEx twice a week to mail a package approximately five miles from where I was living at the time, and he would give me $500 for each trip. I didn't know what was in the package. All I knew was that it was going to the panhandler, who owned the Pac-Man video game machines then. Let me tell you, money can help you get over somebody real quick, But all of this was a trap and the beginning of my *sinkhole* because now this fun had shifted into work. He knew me through my ex and knew my ex sold drugs occasionally, so he allowed me to sell cocaine to the people I was around who were getting high. My ex had to buy his drugs through me instead of him. This allowed me to have money instead of depending on him, and ole boy didn't like that at all.

    This opened the door to me transporting drugs because, after that, I started to travel with him and our friend to Florida to pick up kilos of cocaine. This trip would take 24 hours down and 24 hours back. We would do a turnaround for the purpose of having two drivers. All he did was just ride (using us). We would arrive in Florida, check into a hotel, get something to eat, shower, meet the panhandler, and jump back on the highway. When we met the panhandler, I was amazed by how they would make sure we positioned the car side by side in a parking lot so we could not turn to look at him. We could not describe this man because we never saw his face. I really did enjoy the fast money because the pay for driving was over the top when in reality, I was taking a foolish risk. I started thinking I was a big shot drug dealer.

DECEPTION IS REAL

This didn't last long because a monkey can not sell bananas. I was so deceived to think I was a drug dealer. I never kept any money because all of my profit supported my high and all the other things that went hand in hand with my addiction, such as alcohol, cigarettes, and marijuana. He ended up going to Louisville, Kentucky, for a little while, and there was a guy he introduced me to, and we would hang out. I had moved in with my sister and her husband by this time. The guy I was introduced to would visit. We would play cards, laugh, get high, and just have a good time. I was still traveling with the skin regimen, and they had scheduled me to go and do a demonstration in Louisville, Kentucky. My friend decided to drive me, and I was ok with that. Two nights before we were leaving, I had a dream, which I didn't usually do, that something was going to happen. I dreamed we stopped at a gas station. I went in to use the washroom, and he was sticking up the gas station when I came out. Back in the early 80s, everybody carried a pistol, but I told him if he took his gun, I was not going. He laughed and promised he was not carrying it.

On October 5, 1986, my friend and I headed to Louisville, Kentucky. While I was at the studio doing a demonstration of the skin regimen, my friend met up with him. After the demonstration, he picked me up and took me to see him. We hung out, and right before heading back home, he gave us a package of cocaine for personal use. Then he handed us two large separate packages that contained a large quantity of cocaine (1oz each to be exact), one each for the both of us since he was not going to be coming back to Illinois and we would not see him for a while. My friend's package was for business, and mine was so that I would have money. By this point, I could care less about what dude was doing and who he was doing it with. He was now running up behind me. But in reality, it was only for the drugs and not to be with me, although it felt good to be the other woman and not be the one cheated on. I believe it felt good because the tables had turned. She was looking for him, and he would be with me.

    I had become a petty drug dealer because this high came down faster than it went up. On October 7, 1986, we headed back home. On the way back to Illinois, my friend wanted to carry all the drugs instead of us each taking our own. Before we left Kentucky, I had this bright idea because of the dream I had prior to the trip, and I presented it to him, but like most men, he didn't want to listen because what did I know? I was new to the game. I told him I thought having someone meet us would be common sense. We could drop the product at a road marker and let someone else come and pick it up, or put me in another form of transportation with the product and have someone pick me up. He disagreed, so we rolled out and headed back home. I will never forget the Welcome to Illinois sign. Guess what? As soon as we crossed the state line from Indiana, the State Troopers were lined up at the weigh station waiting on us. I usually sleep on a long road trip unless I'm the one driving, so while he was driving, I slept. He woke me up right before we approached the Welcome to Illinois sign, saying that we were almost home. I let the visor down to freshen up my face, and the State Troopers were the first thing I saw. I asked him what he thought was going on. I had no clue they were waiting for us. He replies, " I don't know, but a car has been following us all the way from Kentucky and has not let anyone get in between us. I'm thinking, dummy, I told you. I was not scared because I automatically knew my story because I had a good alibi. I was in the car because he had taken me to do a product promotion for a skin regimen, which was my job, and if they checked, my story would be the truth.

THE SET UP

As we passed the state line, the highway had been blocked off, State Troopers were everywhere, and traffic was at a dead stop and backed up on the highway. I was totally shocked. Before we knew it there was a police car behind us with lights flashing, and my friend had the nerve to reach under his seat and hand me his gun. He told me to put it in my purse; they would not search me. What did I do like a big dummy? I take the gun from him and put it in my purse. Once they stopped us, Police came from everywhere yelling, "Halt, nobody move! This is one time I could've been dead because the sunroof was open, and a gun was pointed right at me. I reached, turned the music off, and opened the sunroof wider. Don't ask me why, but again, this was one of the times I felt the hedge around me. I knew there was a God right then because they could've blown my head off thinking I was reaching for a gun. They slung the car doors open, threw him on the ground, and slung open my car door. As they pulled me out of the car, I kicked my purse onto the ground, and guess what fell out? Of course, the gun. Now, there were guns pointed at me from every direction. Believe it or not, I wasn't scared. I felt something I couldn't explain was around me as well. I am so grateful God is faithful to His Word of never leaving or forsaking me. I didn't know the scripture then, but I am a witness. He will never leave or forsake you. He always allowed me to feel His presence in my mess. I often think about this particular part of scripture in Psalms 139:8, *If we make our bed in hell He is there,"* because at that time in my life, that's exactly what I was doing, making my bed in hell.

They transported us to Joliet to the State Police headquarters and separated my friend and me as they questioned us. They had pictures of my two friends during our stay in Kentucky, the one that drove me and the one that was left in Kentucky together. Come to find out, that's who they were trying to catch, but he always stayed two steps ahead of them. They came into the room where they were questioning me with pictures of drugs in my luggage and all over the dashboard of the car. My friend had a Bible in the car. The pictures showed cocaine in the Bible. Although there are no boundaries when people do drugs, I've yet to see anyone put cocaine in a Bible. Then they showed me pictures with the gun and cocaine in my purse, trying to scare me into giving them information. I had enough sense to know that snitches get stitches if they live, so I played dumb because the pictures were partial truth. The truth was the gun was not mine, and I stuck to it because that was the truth, and I had told my friend not to bring it, so yeah… it was his, and I had planned on not taking the rap for it. I told the police I didn't know where those pictures came from with that white stuff in my luggage, but it was not mine either. The police would then go to him and tell him I said everything was his, which was not true. I ended up being arrested for possession of cannabis and manufacturing and delivery of a controlled substance, but not the possession of the gun. My bond was $3,500 to walk. The money showed up from our friend, and I was released from jail in twelve hours.

      Did I learn anything? Absolutely not. I fought this case for one year and ended up with a Class 4 felony on my record. The sentence was conditional discharge for 30 months, meaning I could not get into trouble nor be caught anywhere where there were drugs or guns for 2.5 years. Some said that was a slap on the wrist; others said I must've turned state's evidence on my friend. The rumor was he was going to kill me. One day, I received a phone call from my friend from jail, and he reassured me that it was a rumor because I knew nothing to tell on him. He asked me to take the rap for the gun because he was on parole for manslaughter, and the gun charge would send him down the river for a long, long time. I told him no because he should not have carried it, especially after the dream. The attorney I was given was sent to me by someone anonymously, and he was one of the best in town. I do not know who sent him, but he showed up, and I didn't have to pay his retainer. Did I stop getting high and get myself together? Nooooo… not even while I was fighting the case. By this time, my addiction to using and selling drugs had kicked up a notch, and I didn't know it. I strongly believe when God brings you out of something, he means for you to stay out.

Chapter 4

I Couldn't Run Away From Me

I don't quite remember how I was able to relocate, but I received a one-way ticket to New Haven, Connecticut. I got a full-time job in a beauty salon as a hairstylist and worked as a waitress in my cousin's bar at night. Getting hooked up with drugs and drug dealers didn't take long because everything ran through the beauty salon and bar. The salon was next door to a liquor store, where all the drug dealers hung out. I lived with some of my relatives, and eventually, that got old. I moved downtown, which was known as the redlight district on Chapel Street. That's where any and everything was going on in my apartment, and I lost it because I couldn't meet the rent. Although I worked two jobs, bills were definitely not a priority. My high came first. This was a sign that I was back on that rollercoaster again wishing it would stop. During this time I really did not know I could be delivered.

One of my clients thought it would be good for me to change jobs and thought I would be a good candidate for a job in the Community Action Agency working with women on welfare, helping them to find housing and following up with them to make sure the rent was being paid on time. I applied, and I got the job. One of the landlords I was working with offered me a job that came with a perk, which included my own apartment in a 40-unit building to collect his portion of the rent from the tenants that were a part of the Rental Assistance Program. Some tenant portions of the rent were as low as $11 a month. At least twenty of the tenants in the building were in my caseload, and approximately 15 of the 20 tenants were drug addicts and alcoholics. They never slept. I knew some of them from the bar where I waitressed and from running in the same circle of associates, so they knew I got high, and very few knew I would always keep a stash that was enough to share or sell from time to time. This was not good because those who knew of me tried to latch on as my buddies when, in reality, all we had in common was drugs, alcohol, and now me being their caseworker.

It wasn't long before I got the "bright idea" that I could keep enough drugs on hand to sell to a few people I knew right there, and I would not have to leave the building. I could sell a little bit to support my habit. I started selling crack to a few individuals I thought I could trust, and it didn't take long for this to catch up with me. Remember, the sole purpose of placing me in the building was to encourage and motivate the women to pay their rent on time. The women were to bring the rent to me on the first of the month, and I would turn it in to the landlord. For those that didn't, I would go and try to collect it because part of my job was to keep track of who did and did not pay. When I would go to collect the money, my so-called friends were always the ones that would never have their money. Some of their portion of the rent was as low as $11 a month. They had no problem telling me they didn't have the money because they had spent it with me on drugs. What do you think happened when the office would follow up? They told them the same thing they told me.

One day, I came home to my apartment, and the door was kicked in. A notice was on the floor stating my apartment had been raided, but they found nothing. I was distraught. I had just come from a doctor's appointment confirming that I was pregnant. I was shaken up, but not enough to stop selling. I only stopped consuming drugs because the baby wouldn't let me. I lost that job and was also fired from the agency because of the accusations of me selling drugs, and there was no way I was going to fight it.

Once I found out that I was pregnant, I could not use drugs because getting high and drinking would make me really sick. My boyfriend at the time, my daughter's father, had no clue I was using drugs. He thought I was just a drinker and I never had any money because I gambled playing cards. We moved in together, and I thank God my daughter would not allow me to use drugs while carrying her. Because of that, she was born with no drugs in her system. In 1991, they would take your baby and place them in foster care if your baby was born with drugs in their system. After I gave birth to her, it didn't take long for me to return to abusing drugs and alcohol. The progression of my addiction was more intense than before. There is no doubt that once you put drugs or alcohol down and pick it back up, it picks up where it left off, and the addiction gets worse than before. Narcotics Anonymous talks about the progression of the addiction once you pick it back up. The

Bible talks about seven demons returning with the one that left, which meant I had to fight eight.

YOU DON'T NEED A BABY

My mom never wanted me to have children because she worried about something wrong with my babies because of how long I was on drugs. She would say to me, "Don't bring me no deformed grandbabies," and she meant it. Before I had my daughter, my mom moved away and remarried. When my aunts (her sisters) met my baby for the first time, they inspected the baby and gave my mom a report. Glory to God, the report was good: she had all of her limbs, was healthy, clean, and was being well taken care of. It was because she had an awesome father who came more than 100% and took excellent care of his child while I pretended to be functional. I was impregnated with my daughter at 29 and gave birth at 30. I can say this was my first attempt at getting clean, and I succeeded. However, it was not by choice. It was definitely by force because smoking crack and drinking would make me unexplainably sick. When I brought my beautiful baby girl home, I was going out to get my prescription filled (legal and illegal) within two hours. While waiting for the legal prescription to be filled, I would go get a bag of crack, and that was all it took. If you know anything about anyone smoking crack, one is too many, and one thousand is never enough. Instead of quitting while I was ahead, I opened that door again and woke up that sleeping giant. I realized after a couple of days, I could not stop. This was not good… It is a fact once you stop using drugs for any length of time and pick them back up it takes off from where you left off, and the addiction escalates quickly, that is no lie. The progression was insane. Here I go again only this time I have a little one.

The struggle became real because now it takes more work to balance hiding my addiction, working, taking care of a baby, and not looking like what I was doing. I have always had a phobia of my baby being taken because of drugs. That was one of the hardest things I think I have ever had to do. An older lady living in the apartment in front of us would tell me to bring her the baby, and she not only loved my daughter but was allowing me to get the kinks out and hoping I would get it together. Well, as we all know, I did not.

STRAIGHT BUSTED

When my daughter was four years old, things between her dad and me were very strained because he was no longer in the dark about what was happening with me. I remember just like yesterday, I was home taking a long bath (like always when I called myself hiding in the bathroom, sneaking and getting high), and I forgot to lock the bathroom door. He had received some good news and ran into the bathroom to share it with me, and when he turned the knob and opened the door, I had the crack pipe to my lips. Oh my God... that was it for him, there was nothing I could say. Our lease was up, and he decided we had to part ways. So then, I pretended that I wanted to act right, and I even went as far as to go into rehab (not for me, but because I was going to be homeless). After the eighth day, they pulled me out of the group to tell me that my

I MADE IT OUT

insurance would not cover my treatment due to my assessment, which was because I didn't tell the truth when the questions were asked during the evaluation. I was ok with it because I really didn't want to be there anyway, and nobody knew I was being released. While there for those eight days, I could only make one phone call, and when I did make the call, it was to let someone know that I had to leave and the reason.

    I could not reach one family member because they were all gone to bury my grandmother. No one informed me that my grandmother had passed, and the excuse was they didn't want to disturb my treatment. I got out of rehab looking for my baby, only to find out she was in Mississippi with my mom, and I was angry. Prior to going to treatment my daughter's father had agreed to take my daughter until I got out and got myself together, I felt someone should've told me my grandmother had passed. I had left boxes and boxes of clothes and shoes at a friend's house because I had nowhere else to leave them. I had nice, expensive clothing and shoes, enough to dress sixty days in a row and not wear the same thing twice. When I got off the bus in front of the lady's house where I had left my belongings, she was having a yard sale with my clothing and shoes. My clothes were hanging all over the fence on hangers, folded on tables, and my shoes lined up just like they were in a department store, only they were outside. So now I'm left with what was on my back and what was in my bag, which was not much because you are limited to what you can take to rehab. I could not do anything about it because once I called the police, it was her word against mine that those were even my things. If you haven't figured it out by now, my so-called friend was also a drug addict and that's the chance I took. Those were clothes and shoes I purchased with the money I made while transporting drugs like I was a big baller.

Looking back, I was starting to be stripped of everything, and that still was not enough for me to stop using drugs. Another person offered me a room to live in until I could find myself a place to stay. I have always had the ability to hustle (survive) because I had an addiction to drugs and refused to sell my body. That is not to say I have not slept with anyone for drugs because I have to be truthful. After all, it is part of the lifestyle.

Back in the day, I had a couple of nicknames. They would call me Underground because I could and would find it if you wanted it. It would cost you, but I would make it happen. Another name I was given in the streets was Q (which was short for Chiquita), which is my middle name because people in the streets could never pronounce my name right. My mom's sister would always tell me that I needed to get rid of those nicknames because they come with spirits. I hated my name, Cheryl, for absolutely no good reason. I thought it sounded like a white girl; how foolish was that? So, for decades, I never used my name other than on legal documents.

I was going out one Friday night, and someone wanted some VCR tapes. A friend came to take me to sell them to them, and we got stopped by the police for a traffic stop. The cop ran the driver's name, and they came back clean. Then they ran my name, and I had a warrant for my arrest for a traffic violation, so they locked me up. My bond was only $50, and different individuals tried to come and

I MADE IT OUT

bond me out and could not because no one knew my real name. They only knew my street name. I stayed in jail until Monday and was released with no bond because they considered my weekend stay as time served.

Chapter 5

The Sinkhole

There were so many little episodes that I could share about my spiral out of control due to drugs while out on the East Coast from 1988-1997. That sinkhole was no joke; no matter how much I desired it to stop, I just continued to sink. One of the darkest times in my addiction was when I moved in with a friend with my daughter when she was starting Head Start so I could have a stable environment for her. While living there, I decided to try to stop using drugs. Believe it or not, things were going well because, at that point, all I had was me and God to depend on. My daughter inspired me because I wanted to prove that I could care for her. I would have her during the week because her dad worked weekdays, and then he would pick her up on the weekends and keep her until Sunday evening.

One day he picked her up in the middle of the week prior to her starting pre-school to take her to get a book bag and school supplies along with a trip to McDonalds. He picked her up and never brought her back. He kidnapped her. I freaked out and went off. I could not understand why he felt she was not in good hands because as long as I was with him, she was safe, even when I was high, and he was gone. He always told me they were a package. I was getting it together, and where I was living at the time, no one did drugs. I believe he did that because I had started dating someone else.

Sadly, the only way I knew to cope with my daughter being taken (kidnapped in my eyes) was to get high and drink because that's precisely what I resorted to. I moved out of my friend's house and in with the guy I was dating. He was Jamaican, and he was also a drug dealer. I started running back and forth to Harlem to pick up drugs for him. He moved me in my own place and helped me get on my feet. He would constantly say to me, "Star" (the nickname he gave me), you are better than that. You have got to get off them drugs." He didn't find anything wrong with the distribution end of it though.

After a few months of finally being in my own apartment, I got a call that my siblings and I needed to get to Mississippi as soon as possible because my father had surgery and was not doing well. They didn't expect him to make it. The report was my dad had black lung disease and could not talk on the phone because he could not say more than six words without coughing profusely. I called anyway, and they allowed me to speak with him. My dad talked to me for about twenty minutes on December 12, 1996, and did not cough once. I knew right then he was not going to make it. I remember my last conversation with him, and I asked him if he wanted me to be his Christmas present and come visit him? He told me yes and also how much he loved me, which was something he had never said to any of his children, although we knew he loved us. I knew without a doubt that he loved me and I was his favorite. My dad passed on Friday, December 13, 1996, and I was scheduled to depart to Mississippi on the 15th.

    Christmas was my father's favorite holiday. He would light up the whole block with Christmas lights on the house. On the 24th of December, I was on the train on my way home from burying him, which was really hard for me. On my train ride home from Mississippi, all I could think about was his promise to hold on because I told him I wanted to talk. I knew he was passing and needed closure on a few things. What made things ok for me was that he said he loved me. He said it about three times on the phone during our last conversation, and to this day, I can't understand why that was so important because he showed it. He also told me he was sorry, and I was left to wonder about what because we never had the chance to discuss it. I often wonder what that conversation would have been like. I remember visiting my dad with my daughter when she was a baby, and when I was ready to leave to go back to Connecticut, he said, "Tell me, why is it when my children have money, they don't stop until they give it to the drug dealers?" I was shocked because I thought I was hiding what I did from him.

    I don't remember my dad going to church or considering himself saved. He was a hard worker, and worked two full-time jobs all my life, along with owning two businesses at two different times in my life. I remember him having a drink every day, and I never saw him drunk. I heard he gave his life to the Lord a few months before he passed, and I was given his Bible, which I have today.

I MADE IT OUT

My three siblings and I inherited his house not long after my dad passed. Two of my siblings and I moved back in the house together in Joliet, Illinois, where we grew up. My baby brother lived in upstate New York. That was a huge mistake, and it was also the beginning of my *manhole*. We inherited a four-bedroom house with no mortgage, and the party was on. I only had one child (my daughter) at the time, and my sister had three children, and there was plenty of room in this ranch style home that we grew up in. It was nothing but a party that never stopped. My brother was a truck driver, so he was in and out. My sister and I stayed home and did what we wanted to do, and that was get high. Different ones were in and out all hours of the day and night. Our drug and alcohol addiction robbed us of our inheritance. On top of our addiction, there was a lack of knowledge of how to handle responsibilities and take care of our business regarding owning a home. Sadly, we smoked up our house and ended up losing it. We were out of control.

My mom's husband passed away in May 1999, and she had gotten wind of what was going on down on Edward Street (the street we grew up on and were living) residing. There was always a lot of traffic in and out of our house, and one day she showed up. She came to rescue her grandchildren, and the invitation was open to my sister. I took it upon myself to tag along. We were both full-blown drug addicts and alcoholics, and she made it clear she didn't come to get me. Still, from time to time, she made sure I understood that. For some reason, our relationship has always been strained, and no matter how hard I tried to win my mother over, it just didn't seem to happen.

I love my mother with everything in me, and I have always admired her to the point that everything she did and was I wanted to be and do. For example, she was a hairstylist, so I went to cosmetology school to become a stylist. She went to school to become a surgical nurse. I went to school and became a Nursing Assistant. She was a good mother, and although I was bound in addiction, I desired to be a good mother. We always seemed to clash, but when things between us were good, it was really good.

    I have always felt like the black sheep of my family. I was always told that was not the case; each child had different needs, and I was the one they didn't have to worry about because I would make it. I also believe I was treated differently because I was rebellious, resentful, and angry because I was carrying that deep, dark secret alone, not knowing how to release it because I thought no one would believe me.

    My sister and I and our children moved to Bolingbrook in 1999, and I found out that I was pregnant before moving. Again, I was very ill and could not continue using drugs or drinking alcohol. I was trying hard to hide the pregnancy, and eventually, I could not hide it any longer because I had become too sick. I had made the decision not to keep the baby until after about the fifth month of pregnancy because the report after various tests was at the age of 38, my race and blood type (which is rare and no one ever said anything about until my second pregnancy) I ranked 1 out of 8 to have a Down Syndrome baby. All I could think about was my mother's words, "You don't need a baby because you have been doing drugs too long. Don't bring me a retarded grandbaby." The fact that I had given birth to a healthy, beautiful baby girl didn't even register; instead, those words brought on fear. I was so fearful that I was stressed throughout the pregnancy. After numerous ultrasounds, I discovered it was a boy I had always wanted. Still, I could not see myself caring for a special needs child, so I contemplated adoption because I knew I could not have another abortion since I had already had two.

 My brother, who lived in upstate New York, found out I was considering giving the baby up for adoption, and he begged me not to. He promised if I would keep the baby, he would help me. He would say, "What if nothing is wrong with him? Then, you will have to deal with the baby looking for you and wondering why he was given up for adoption." So I decided to keep the baby, and my brother kept his word and made sure I didn't need anything. I stayed clean throughout the pregnancy, and they kept running series of tests to ensure the baby had all his limbs and organs intact. On November 19, 1999 I gave birth to the most beautiful baby boy in the world and he was healthy.

 With the ability to go through my pregnancies clean after finding out early I was pregnant gave me hope that I could get off drugs. I could not understand why I could not do it once the babies were born. I knew that the real reason I was able to do it was not willpower it was pregnancy sickness which was horrible. I remember looking into my babies faces as newborns and it would hurt me to my core the look that was in their eyes. They would look at me as to say, "Why do you do that"? I knew I looked different to them when I was high because of the facial expressions they would make. In their eyes was sadness, which crushed me, but I could not stop using drugs and drinking, knowing nothing on this earth meant more to me than my babies. I still could not stop for them and did not understand why. I would often reflect on how easy it was to stop using when I was pregnant, like it was not by choice when I knew the only reason I could take a break was because it made me so sick.

After having my son I would come up with every excuse in the book to get a few minutes out away from the house so I could go and purchase my drugs and make a stop at one of the crack houses in the area to get high. It became too much work so I started sneaking and getting high in the house. I would come home frustrated and angry because it was a waste of time and money. People would love to see me running in those crack houses for those few minutes because they knew I was sneaking and they could and would get what was left in the pipe because I would be too paranoid to leave out of their house with it. It was nothing to be stopped by the police once exiting some of those houses.

This behavior caused issues at home because there was an excessive amount of time spent in the bathroom. That was the only place in the house that I could have privacy. This became work because now I had to hide the smell and make sure I didn't leave any paraphernalia behind (which I did often). There was constant chaos and confusion because this wasn't something I did alone. I had a partner in crime who lived under the same roof, so this would cause constant arguments and verbal fights over who would get the most and be rushed out of the bathroom. I thought that was strange because I was the one with the hustle, and they felt they were entitled to what I had, so to keep the peace, I would give the drugs away. I've always given away more drugs than I smoked to maintain peace or to be able to smoke what I had in alone. So why couldn't I stop?

While living with my mom, she would leave for work in the afternoon around 2 p.m., and we would have one big party after she left. People were coming in and out bringing drugs so that my sister and I (along with my brother when he was in town) could purchase them, or we would be purchasing them. My mom's house had become known as a crack house in the neighborhood, and my sister and I had been labeled crackheads. At one time, the police would sit outside the house down the street and stop individuals leaving our house, trying to catch them with something, so I started selling drugs because I was usually the main one running in and out, buying drugs for people anyway. Another reason I would keep enough drugs on me to sell was because it would keep me with product, and I could make sure if there was anything needed for my children, I would always have a few dollars on hand. I had a phobia of being labeled as a non-fit mother. However, I was as non-fit as they came. The worst feeling in the world was my babies needing something to eat after I had sold the food stamps and I couldn't provide. I constantly feared my children being taken from me through Children and Family Services because of my drug addiction, but it wasn't enough for me to quit. That baffled me because I just could not stop.

There was a police officer who patrolled our neighborhood that my son just adored. He wanted to become a police officer like him. My son would break away from me when we would be outside to say hello to him. At

Christmas time, this particular police officer would come and bring a big box of toys for my son. When Mr. Officer saw me, he always asked, "What you doing, Q? Stay out of trouble." I know without a shadow of a doubt my son was the reason I never got busted. I would always say my son has saved me from being thrown under the penitentiary because I lived as though I had nine lives. My drug addiction was out of control, and I knew it.

I will never forget the time I had been out all night, and I had come home early afternoon because I had a job interview, I came home to get a bath and get dressed. My mom was in her sewing room sewing, my children were at school (no, I was not there to get them up and off to school), and right after I had run my bath water and got undressed, there was a knock at the door.

My mom yelled upstairs and said, "Quita (that was also one of my nicknames), there is someone here to see you," and I yelled back, "Who"? And she said it's the police, and I said, "Quit playing." I went to the door, and guess what? It was three policemen, and because I knew them, their exact words were, "You have to go with us, Q," They told me that they had a warrant for my arrest and would give me the details when we got to the police station. Again, I said to them, "Quit playing," but in the back of my mind, I said to myself, "It is three of them. What have I done?" They didn't handcuff me; they walked me to the car, read me my rights, and put me in the front seat of the police car while one drove to the police station and the other two rode in the back seat without saying a word. When we got to the police station, I was placed in a room to be interrogated concerning drugs and guns. They insisted I was running the

I MADE IT OUT

drugs in Bolingbrook, Illinois. I was surprised because I knew they knew I was a crack addict. My life was becoming darker and darker, and my hole was becoming deeper and deeper.

    The MANS Agents had been building a case (investigating) for six months, and on this particular day, they did a sting and rounded up 27 people. I was not afraid. All I wanted to know was where they got their information that I was a drug dealer and where were they parked to know I had come home. What they did was my son's friend Officer A (the one that was friends with my baby boy) had been sitting outside my house for hours waiting for me to come home because he had stopped by the house earlier and left a business card with my mom for me to call him and he knew I would think nothing of it and call. Well, that's exactly what I did, and there was no answer, but as soon as I hung the phone up, there was a knock at the door.

    Boy, were they upset to find out that I was a drug user and not a big-time distributor. One officer had the nerve to call me a queen pen. They insisted I sold drugs, and truth be told, I understood why because I was in and out, running back and forth to get the drugs because others using with me and around me were too paranoid to go. So, I would run and buy the drugs for them, which was one of the ways I supported my habit. This is when I learned that you could be charged as a distributor when drugs are exchanged from one hand to another. This is why I called myself a petty drug dealer because I was taking risks that, at 46 at the time of this arrest, would and could cost me everything, including my children. God allowed me to get away with my mess for all those years, and I was not satisfied until I ran into that dead end my mother often had warned me about.

After about 13 hours in the holding cell, I was transported to Will County Jail in Joliet, Illinois. While being transported, I told myself I would no longer use. I spent sixty-six long days in the county jail. Those were the longest days of my life; all I could think about was I had to do something different. I had to change my life because I had been exposed. I was so embarrassed to be arrested in the presence of my mother. This is where I took my first Bible study course, and I took it very seriously because there was nothing else to do. In jail, there was nothing to do but eat, or sleep, and the food was horrible. We could only shower every other day, and if we were on administrated lockdown, we were locked in our cell for up to 23 hours at a time (caged like an animal) and playing cards.

I received one visit outside of the two visits from my public defender. That visit was from one individual that God had assigned to my life. He told me that he was sent to help me see where my life was headed because he could hear the cry down on the inside that I desired to be free from drugs. He would tell me he could hear the cry because he had been there and knew the struggle. Out of the blue, he would call at the right time to encourage me and tell me that I could overcome, too, and he would be willing to help me to walk it out. It was almost like the story of the man who was drowning and crying out to God for help. God sent the life jacket, boat, and helicopter, and the man still drowned. When he got to Heaven, he asked God what took him so long? God replied, "I sent help there three times:

I MADE IT OUT

remember the life jacket, boat, and helicopter that showed up? That was me. God had sent numerous people to help me, and I would shun them away because the bottom line was part of me was not ready, and I didn't have the heart to own up to that. I waited until I was 46 to get a Class 4 felony for Manufacturing and Delivery of a Controlled Substance (Cannabis/marijuana) and go to jail. How pathetic was that? God had given me a chance after chance to deal with my addiction and not have any trouble with the police.

I know God gave me grace with the police. They had plenty of opportunities to shut me down. I will never forget the day they pulled up to my house. They came from everywhere. When they pulled up, I saw they were getting ready to raid my mom's house. They came to ask my daughter to play on their basketball team because she was just that good. The open vision was a sign my mess was getting old.

After sixty-six long days in the county jail, on May 8, 2008, I was charged with distribution of narcotics and selling to an undercover officer. This was considered a third transaction. I didn't hand it to the officer; I had made a run to purchase drugs for someone who was setting me up. I was released from the county jail and placed on probation with conditions because I had no other recent convictions. I had to report to my probation officer every two weeks for five years and give urine samples. Once they assessed me, they realized I was a drug addict, not a drug dealer. I despised meeting my probation officer and walking a tightrope in the beginning. Still, I realized that he was strategically sent to save my life at the end of my probation period. I met with him twice a week, and he decided that I should go to an outpatient drug and alcohol program. I didn't have a problem with going to the program, but the place I was referred to was surrounded by drug dealers who were posted outside waiting for the people to come out of the meetings. So I told my probation officer I was not going, and I didn't. I did well for approximately 4-5 months because I took the advice and changed where I went and who I hung out with.

I applied for a job, went to work, came home, and cared for my children, which became my daily routine for a short while. On my off days, it became a struggle because what would I do with my time while the children were in school and people were still ringing the doorbell because they knew I was home? They could care less about me trying to comply with the rules set through my terms and agreement with probation. They wanted to get high, and they either didn't know where to purchase the drugs or were too afraid to buy them on their own. For me, it was a setup from the devil. They would give me money and ask me to get them drugs, and they were very happy to pay me to go because they knew they didn't have to share. With absolutely no tools to walk this thing out, I started thinking that just because it has been 3-4 months, I could handle going to purchase drugs for them and not want any for myself. The drug dealers were surprised to see me; believe it or not, they didn't want to sell the drugs to me. Before getting arrested and being placed on probation, they always asked me when I would get off the drugs because I was better than that. They would say that but didn't stop taking the money and never turned me away.

I did well for a short period of time, and one day,

when I was in a storm, meaning all hell had broken loose at home, there was a ring at the door. It was right on time, and I don't mean right on time for me to open the physical door because someone was on the other side of it, but right on time because of my emotions of anger. It was the perfect time for the enemy to creep back in. I was in a really bad place, so I said forget it. I went and got the drugs, took the money the individual paid me, and purchased me a bag, too. I gave in to my emotions and got high. Did I give into my emotions, or did I use the issue that was going on at home at that particular moment as an excuse because I had reservations in the back of my mind? I am going to be honest and say I used the situation as an excuse because I know my abstinence from using drugs was by force and not by choice again. The arrest, which led to probation and the fear of going to the penitentiary, was my real reason for being able to abstain from using drugs for as long as I did. I didn't have to stop drinking, so I found myself substituting the drugs for more consumption of the alcohol. I drank more than I ever did and drank to get drunk.

This was one of the biggest mistakes I ever made, opening that door to smoking crack cocaine again. The Bible talks about how the enemy goes away for a season; he goes out into dry places seeking rest, and when he can't find rest, he returns to see if the house is clean. If it is not, he brings seven more worse than the one that left. The progression of my addiction picked up where it left off, and oh my God, it didn't take long before I was out of control. Things got so bad that my mom had enough and told me I had to move. Her exact words were, "I don't know what you need, but I do know I can't help you, and don't come back to this house until you get some help because I can't take it no more." There was something about the way she said it that particular time. I knew she meant every word she was saying. It hurt me because I knew I was sick and had nowhere to go. Where am I going to go? After constantly telling her I had somewhere to go when she would threaten to put me out. I had the nerve to ask her, "What about my children?" The answer was, "What about them? You were here and didn't care, so why are you concerned about them now?"

It baffled me how my addiction shifted into turbo mode so fast. It took off like a car in the NASCAR race. I was holding on for dear life as I came to grips with the fact that I can't stop. Here I was, back off the races. Being ejected from my mom's house was the most devastating thing I had to endure besides being molested because I was a drug addict and could not take care of my children. See, the whole time, I was deceiving myself that I could take care of my children, but in reality, my mom took care of my children, and my daughter's father did his part in taking care of her.

I ended up living in a place I could not get enough of as long as I didn't have to live there, which was the CRACK HOUSE. One of my associates lived in a house where I was allowed to come and smoke crack. Now that I was put out of my mom's house with nowhere to go, I was offered a place to stay because I was the one with the drugs most of the time, and if not, I could get them. This became a disaster because everybody would sleep or have an attitude when there were no drugs. I am not exactly sure how long this went on. All I know is it went on long enough for me to end up in a worse state than the one I was in. I longed for God to bring me out of it. My addiction got so bad that I would walk down the street on my way to meet the drug dealers, praying and asking God to please deliver me. I would be in the crack house desperate for change, smoking the crack pipe and crying please, God help me. I would get so overwhelmed that I would put on gospel music, which would freak everybody out. They wanted me to turn it off or get out because it would blow their high. I would say, "Turn it off? We need God to keep us through this." I started becoming so paranoid when I would get high that I needed gospel music to calm me down. It was something about gospel music; I would play "Imagine Me" by Kurt Franklin over and over. Believe it or not, that song helped me to see myself delivered, not just stopping but free.

The lady who allowed me to stay in her home, her mom, lived across the street and was a Pastor at the time. She knew every time one of us would leave out of the house, when we would return, as well as when someone would pull up to sell us drugs. Sometimes, I would bump into her on my way to meet my children, which was around the corner, and she would always say to me, "Q, take your will to live back." I would ask her how do I do that, and she would say, Q, you have to make a conscious decision that you will not live like that. I would hear those words in my sleep without knowing how to do it. I knew I was at a point of no return. I started crying out to God, "If you are who people say you are, please help me get off these drugs," because I just knew I would die like that. Thoughts would go through my head of dying of an overdose, and my mother, along with my children, would be embarrassed. I didn't want to hurt them, but I was out there bad.

On the outside, it looked like I did not care about anything and anyone, but on the inside, I was screaming, "Somebody, help me, please." I'm drowning and it seemed no one could see that. Once I would come down off the high, my mood would be so low. Not realizing that by this time, everything I had been through was pushed so far down that I was just angry, bitter, resentful, and nasty to everyone but my children. I would share with different family members how I needed help, and their response would be, "No, you don't just make up your mind. You are going to stop and do it." I didn't understand this thing was bigger than me, and if it was that easy, I would have done it long ago. That, of course, would make me angrier; why couldn't they see it?

Chapter 6

The Turnaround

My addiction had escalated to a point where I would see spirits in the dark; they were real. I knew then crack was going to be the death of me, or I was going to end up in the penitentiary because by now, my urine samples were coming up positive, and I was told if I had one more dirty drop, I was off to the Dept. of Corrections. After that, I learned to drink lots of vinegar so I would drop clean. Nevertheless, I was still threatened with being sent to the penitentiary because now the urine was so white and was registering inconclusive, which meant it was being tampered with, so now all eyes were on me to slip. I knew I had to do something different. I was angry now because there was no way I was going to the penitentiary, and there seemed to be no way I could stop smoking. By this time, selling was not an option because the grip of addiction was on, and this monkey could no longer sell the bananas. It had become work to get high, whether that meant running for every Tom, Dick, and Harry so I could get a puff or even sleep with someone I knew I would've never slept with if it wasn't for the drugs.

One Sunday afternoon, I went to see my children at

my mom's house, and I had to visit them from the street. I was not allowed on her porch. I would ring the doorbell anyway, and when I would show up, whoever would answer the door (usually one of the children) would come outside on the porch and talk with me. Well, this particular day, my sister's boyfriend, who happened to be Muslim then, came out and spoke with me. He shared how they all (he, my sister, my son, and her children) had gone to church that morning. I asked what the message was about, and he explained it to me and said he enjoyed it and was looking forward to going next Sunday. I was shocked.

The following Saturday, I called the house early enough to ask if I could go with them to church the next day, and they said yes. Don't think people didn't come out of the woodworks wanting me to run and get drugs for them to smoke on Saturday night. They were so generous with what they paid me to get their drugs and shared with me what they purchased to smoke for themselves. I got high with them all night, which I rarely did with these individuals. I would run until I moved into the crack house. It got to where I would tell myself I could not continue doing this. I have to do something different. I've got to get up and go to church. I can't continue to live like this. All I could think about was my son and how he looked forward to me going with them tomorrow, and I couldn't let him down. I made sure, in between my hits off the pipe, that I would lay out the clothes I would wear so I could make sure I looked presentable and not look like I had been up smoking and drinking all night into the wee hours of the morning.

On Sunday morning, the alarm went off, and I

wanted to roll over and go back to sleep (because I had just laid down at around 4 a.m. and dosed off into a really good sleep around 6 a.m.) I jumped up, got into the shower, and got dressed. I went down the street around the corner to meet them for church service. The Pastor pulled up In a Cadillac, and we all piled into the car. It was so many of us that every lap in the car had someone on it. I was so tired and hungover, smelling like malt liquor beer and stale cigarette smoke.

    Church service was held at the town Park District gym, and I thought that was good because it wasn't so intimidating. When I entered the gym where the service was held, something happened that I can't explain, but the message was about faith. After the message, right before the offering, the Pastor did an altar call and called me up. When I came forth, he prophesied to me, and God showed this man (Pastor) things that had taken place in my life and things I had done the night before coming to church. In my ear, the Pastor rewound my life like a movie, saying God loved me. He told me how God would send me back to get others who were just like me and win them to the Kingdom of God. He shared how God had a plan for my life; I believe that's what I left the church service with. Despite all the mess I had made of my life, God still loved me and wanted to use me. He told me how God heard me whenever I cried out to Him to help me because I didn't want to live like that anymore. I knew from that moment on God was real. I didn't care what anyone said or thought. That moment blessed my life because that's exactly what I'd done, cried out, saying I didn't want to live like that anymore.

    The time came for the Pastor to drop me off at the

crack house where I lived. I asked if I could go next Sunday, and the answer was yes. Did I stop getting high? No, but I felt horrible (which I now understand as conviction) every time I purchased and smoked crack. I couldn't wait for Sunday to get here only for my sister to tell me there was no room in the car that Sunday so I didn't go. On the following Sunday, I didn't ask permission to go with them. I got up to be ready because I knew when he picked them up. I knew where I could stand and see the Pastor no matter which direction he was coming to pick them up. As I was walking down the street, I saw the Pastor as he was passing me up, and I yelled out. He pulled over, and I ran, jumped in the car, and told him that I was on my way to meet them to go to church. You should've seen their faces when Pastor pulled up, and I was already in the car. They didn't want to be crowded, and I didn't want to be left behind.

Something happened when I entered the church and I knew I had to get there no matter what. There was a sense of peace, and I felt safe there because I would get something to apply to my life for the week that helped me to see myself off the drugs. I just didn't know how it was going to get done. I wanted out of that lifestyle so badly that I sincerely started to cry out to God without any shame of who knew it. I would smoke and cry, cry and smoke, saying, help me, God, because I had spiraled into a place. I was looking at going back to jail. I couldn't stand being away from my children, I wanted to be a productive member of society therefore I knew I had to do something. It seemed like when I started going to church, the enemy turned up the heat.

I asked the Pastor if he could pick me up on the way

to get the others from then on, and he made sure I had a ride. I thank God he sent different individuals to pick me up, and I would be ready. On Sunday, the Pastor testified how he got delivered from drug addiction. On that particular Sunday, I was the last to get dropped off, and I remember sitting outside my mom's house in the car with him after everyone else had gotten out of the car, and he shared how Jesus was the only way out. He gave me tools, which was scripture to not only meditate on but to speak over myself. He did everything in his power to keep me close until I was able to fly. He and his wife would pray for me and pray with me. Finally, I told them that I was on probation and felt I needed to go into treatment.

    I got the guts to tell my probation officer that I needed treatment after all the times I was telling him I was not using. I had to come clean because I knew at any minute this thing was getting ready to make a real fool out of me, so I concluded I better ask for help. My probation officer gave me a list of places to call and encouraged me to get help because he didn't want to lock me up. He didn't make me give a urine sample on this particular day because I was honest. He planned to escort me right from his office to the jail across the street if I was dirty another time. I ran quickly and found a treatment center. I called The Share Program and did the assessment over the phone, and within two days, they called me back and told me to come right now; they had a bed for me. I was happy but, in the midst of getting high, so I told the lady on the phone I could not come right at that time because I had to situate my children and get a babysitter. The lady told me God was the best babysitter and I needed to come now if I wanted the bed. I told the lady I can't come right now. I felt so bad because I had just lied on my children because they were home with my mother. I couldn't enjoy the high for thinking about possibly going to the penitentiary for crack. I think it was at that moment that I really realized that crack was coming before everything, even my freedom.

I woke up the following day, called the treatment center, and told them who I was and that my children were situated. They told me there was no bed available. I cried; boy did I cry. I was told to call every day until a bed opened up. So I called every day, but in the meantime, I continued to get high. The previous weekend, the disability checks were distributed, which was the real reason I lied on my children because it was like Christmas when the checks came out. Everybody wanted to get high but was too paranoid to go get the drugs themselves. But not Ms. Q; I would run so much that I would earn extra drugs from the drug dealers. They loved seeing me come with the people's money. This was the first of the month, and it went on consistently until the fourth of every month when everybody's money was gone. I would always have a stash of a few dollars or some drugs hidden for myself for later.

I will never forget August 4, 2009, because I ran and ran (I called it a marathon) for four days, and on the fourth night, around 12:30 a.m., once everyone had run out of money, I was going to call the drug dealer and have him bring something for me. He said to meet him on Buckeye Street in twenty minutes. As I prepared to go meet him I sat on the end of my bed and proceeded to put on my shoes. I put the first shoe on, and when I lifted my other foot, I heard an audible voice saying, "If you go out of that door, you will not return alive." It scared me. I was looking around, and no one was there but me. I cried so hard because I knew I was not freaking out. I heard what I heard. I took those shoes off so fast and went to bed, and all I could hear was, "Let it go, that thing that has you bound." I had gone to church on New Year's Eve 2008, and that was the message. The very next day, the drug dealer called me very upset and cursed me out because there was a shootout between two rival gangs when he pulled up to the designated spot to meet me. For a minute, he thought I had set him up because I wasn't there waiting on him, which was abnormal. I broke down because that was confirmation that God was real, and that voice I heard was God. Some people say God does not speak in an audible voice, but He did then.

Of course, just like the devil, the very next morning, I received a phone call from one of my friends who wanted me to make a run and get them a bag of crack. I got up and made a phone call to a drug dealer and was ready when she pulled up. I went to get her the drugs, and when she was dropping me back off, she told me she wasn't giving me any, and I went off. I started yelling at her to never call me again because I would not run to get her anything else. I was yelling, I'm done; I'm done. She looked me in my eyes, and said these exact words to me, "B#%&@, YOU WILL NEVER STOP SMOKING CRACK!" That's how far out there I was. I used to say I was out there like a let out couch.

I went in the house, and I called the Pastor and shared what had just taken place, and he prayed for me. He didn't condemn me. I then shared with him about the treatment center and how I needed a change of environment because I couldn't do it anymore. He asked if there was anywhere I could go where they didn't do drugs until I could get into a treatment center, and my response was no, because everyone I associated with did drugs and drank.

Someone took me out to eat at Cheddars, and this lady came up to me to tell me one of my old friends, whom I had not seen in a really long time, had lost her mother. She told me to take her number because she would love to hear from me. I had not spoken with her in years, but after we left the restaurant, I could not rest. I felt as though I should call her, so I did. When she picked up the phone, I gave her my condolences, and when I was ready to hang up, she asked me if I wanted to come over and catch up. I told her yes because I knew she did not get high. Glory to God, she was the ram in the bush. We got together, and once I told her what I had been going through and how I was living in a crack house, she replied to me, "I know," because she knew the house when she picked me up. She offered me to stay with her until a bed in the treatment center opened up, but I had to call the treatment center every day to check to see if a bed was available. I ended up staying with her for approximately two weeks.

On this particular Saturday, the people at the treatment center told me to call in the morning, and there should be a bed available, which was Sunday. I called the Pastor and his wife and shared the information with them, and they offered to take me to the center after church.

Before going to church, I called the center, and they said no bed was available, and I was disappointed. By this time, I had a couple of days clean but started having a desire to get high. After church, the Pastor came outside. He and his wife were ready to take me to the treatment center, and I had to tell them there was no bed. People were dispersing to their cars, and he rounded everybody up to come back and agree as he prayed for a bed to open up within 24 hours. I called the treatment center on Monday morning bright and early, and a bed was available. This shook my whole life because I was on my way to change. During the conversation, I shared with the lady on the phone how I had been struggling to stay clean and had done pretty well. She then asked how many days had it been with nothing in my system. By this time, it had been almost three weeks. She explained that if there was nothing in my system when I got there, they would turn me away. So I went and got myself a six-pack of Malt Liquor and drank all of them on the way to the treatment center. By the time of my arrival, I knew I would qualify for that bed because I was drunk, and it didn't take long to get drunk because my system was somewhat cleaned out.

 I stayed in treatment for twenty-eight days, and during that time, I learned about the life and death of drug addiction and the theory behind what I was doing to my body. They helped me to see that I was a dressed up garbage can (that's a term used often when one thinks they are hiding what they are doing) because I spent a lot of time thinking I was hiding what I was doing out of fear of my children being taken from me. I was taught that alcohol was compared to ethyl, which is lead that is used in gasoline. I remember the day I stopped and said to myself, only a fool would walk up to a gas pump and pour a glass of gas to drink. To me, that was something to think about. They also showed us different brains on drugs and alcohol, which looked like Swiss cheese. I truly believe the theory is what impacted me the most, and I am so grateful for the information. I firmly believe that when we know better, we do better. I also heard more than once a day how important it was that we get everything we could out of our time spent there in treatment because our life depended on it.

I walked away grateful to be alive because the first news I received once I got out of treatment was that the lady I went and purchased crack for (the one that wouldn't give me any after I went to cop for her) had died on her bathroom floor smoking crack while I was away. Her last words to me repeated themselves in my thoughts. But here I am only by the grace of God. Today, I am fourteen years free, without a hiccup, as of 2023. Holy Spirit has been my keeper, and I know without a shadow of a doubt who kept me.

Before leaving treatment, I had nowhere to go, but I knew I could not return to the same environment I had just left. I had to change everything. There were no beds available in the halfway houses in my area, so I went to Serenity House and explained the fear of going back home because there were people who were still using drugs and drinking. They could do nothing for me but insist I stay connected to a strong support group. After the knowledge I gained about what I was doing, I didn't want to be the one out of three people to relapse. While in treatment, they would tell us that, according to statistics, one out of three would not stay clean. A lady came into the office and overheard me telling her they had to do something because I couldn't return to where I had come from. She pulled me into what looked like a big closet and interviewed me because she was over the three-quarter houses, which was the last stop before transitioning back out into society. God blessed me to skip the halfway house by moving on her heart and allowing me to occupy one of those beds. She wanted to see how I could get through one week of staying clean and call her the following Monday. I rushed and phoned one of my friends from the streets who was working an honest program through Narcotics Anonymous and asked her if I could stay with her for a week until I could get into a recovery home. She responded, "Absolutely." If we could get high together, we could surely recover and stay clean together. It was like God had her positioned to help me.

  I was serious about pursuing this Jesus that I had started learning about and who was showing Himself strong through little things. He was proving to me that He was real, and my faith was constantly increasing. He was showing me that it was all worked out, and all I had to do was surrender. My Pastor's wife helped me to get the things I needed so that I would not be a burden on anyone and drove me to my friend's house. After seven days, I called, and the lady over the three-quarter house had me come to the office to give a urine sample, and I dropped clean. I was allowed to move into the transition home in Naperville, Illinois, and I have been running for my life ever since. God had a plan.

  There were rules to live in this particular house: you had to find a job within a certain amount of time. There were chores, and you had to attend three 12-Step meetings weekly, get a sponsor, work the twelve steps, and pay rent weekly. Well... I stand here to tell you I am known as the only individual who has entered into Serenity House Transition Housing and has been allowed to have church and Bible study as my meetings, with my pastor and his wife as my sponsors. I am also proud to say instead of working a 12-Step program, they accepted the fact that I took one step to Jesus. As for the rent, until I found a job, a church around the corner did something they had never done in the church's history; they paid $2000 toward my rent. I was told to apply for assistance to get help to pay my rent because they helped the ladies with giving $250 towards their stay. The church informed me that the Lord put it on their heart to pay that amount. At that time, none of that made sense to me. All I could relate to was God was proving himself to me in a way so I would know He was real.

    Many days, I struggled in my mind that I could stay drug and alcohol-free. I remember walking to the bus stop daily not knowing how to pray, but saying to God, "The Bible says if any man be in Christ, he is a new creation; old things have passed away and all things have become new" (2 Corinthians 5:17). I would say, I'm struggling in my mind I keep thinking about getting high. I need you to walk with me, run with me, and, if necessary, carry me through this day, and he did! The struggle was real. I know it was because I had more time on the side of addiction and using drugs than being clean and sober. Whenever there was any pressure due to something not going my way, the first place my mind would go was to use drugs. I would have to immediately go and rewind the tape of how I ended up where I was and reach for the tools I had learned to cope with.

I MADE IT OUT

I resided in Serenity House (the three-quarter house) for eighteen months. God allowed me to bypass the halfway house. This part of rehabilitation was for those who had completed every part of treatment and were ready to transition back into society. I went to church every time the doors were open. I would be one of the first ones there and one of the last ones to leave. I was like a ball and chain to my Pastor and his wife. I was determined to stay clean and saved, although it was a struggle in my mind. However, the more I got into the Word of God and learned how to make the scriptures personal by adding my name to particular scriptures related to me and my journey, the easier it became. I acted on what I believed and learned I had power and authority. I learned to cast down my thoughts. I gained tools and applied them.

I ended up being a peer leader over the house. I made sure the rules were followed, chores were assigned, and people were doing what was expected. I was also responsible for dropping individuals after they returned from home visits when they were under the influence of drugs or alcohol. I began to think that God certainly has a sense of humor for putting me in that position. Finally, after 18 months, it was time to leave the program I had completed. It was time to go and apply everything I had learned and step up to the plate to take care of my children. And release my mom from the false burden of taking care of my children that she had been raising. It was one of the scariest things I had to do because everything about me had changed. I was getting lots of practice on the weekends when I would come home to visit. I believe it was also scary for my mom because I had never really taken 100% care of them because I always had her to fall back on.

    Nevertheless, I was determined to get that right, too. God is so merciful. He restored everything concerning my life, especially my relationship with my children and mom. God restored my life, finances, credit, relationships, peace, and joy. Don't get me wrong, it wasn't magic. I had to do the work. Guilt and shame worked overtime to keep me from moving forward, and all I could do was meditate on Ecclesiastes 9:11, "The race is not given to the swift, nor the battle to the strong, but to those that endured until the end."

    I didn't realize how much of a responsibility it was to be a full-time mom. I sure would've done things differently if I knew what I know now. I loved every moment of it, but when it was time to finally move into my own place, which was something I had never done because the only time I lived away from home was with a boyfriend. I remember hearing God say, "Go back home and help your mother by paying her rent out of honor because she has always helped you." He also had a plan to restore our relationship, which took a lot of work and perseverance because we both had done a lot of damage. I needed to forgive, as well as be forgiven. I learned that forgiveness isn't for the other person but for you. I wanted God to forgive me for everything I had done, so who was I not to forgive anyone else? I couldn't change my mom or anyone else. I had to stay focused on myself and what I was supposed to do: walk in forgiveness. I can say forgiving my mom for what I thought was wrong treatment turned out to be what I needed, which was tough love. She stopped enabling me. She wanted me to stay in the lives of my children, but there came a time when she had to make a decision because my being around was a disservice to them. So, although I feel there were a lot of things said and done to me to cause pain, I had to be willing to move past the petty stuff and be willing to do what was in the best interest of us all, and that was learn to forgive. No, it wasn't easy; it was work.

God wanted me to move back home. My daughter was in high school and on her way to college. My son was an honor roll student all through school and never opened a book. He was very smart, a drummer in the school band, and a part of a traveling drumline. I found out later that's how he dealt with his emotions and everything that was going on around him by beating his drums. My daughter buried herself in sports. God told me to come and adjust to their world and be mindful that uprooting him from his environment would cause a terrible disruption because we would be moving to a different school district. He would have to make new friends, and it would derail him. It took a lot of courage to say I was going to do what was in the best interest of my children because I must admit my life had always been what was best for me. I continued to do the work and handle my responsibilities. I couldn't just go away because I had changed and was no longer doing drugs. I had to continue to do the work in the environment where so much damage had been done. When the road would get rough, I had to learn how to push through and not go back to what was familiar, which was fleeing thoughts of using drugs. I will say it again: IT WAS A LOT OF WORK, but here I am on the other side. We made it. I could not have ever gotten where I am today without first making a conscious decision that I was going to do whatever it took to heal and be restored.

Chapter 7

I Am A Miracle, Sign & Wonder

I am no longer that person whom you previously read about in the earlier chapters. I am continuing to heal and be responsible for my actions. Let me sum up what was really going on.

I was broken in more ways than one. I was a little girl suffering in silence, carrying a deep, dark secret that she didn't think anyone would believe or not blame her for. I was scared, wounded, and ashamed.

My pain was very, very loud, and still, to this day, it baffles me that no one could see that I was hurting. All they saw was the fruit of my pain, which was anger, resentment, meanness, and rebellion. But on the inside, she was screaming for help. This deep, dark secret caused me to have very low self-esteem. I felt unworthy and was full of shame and guilt. I hated myself, and it made me feel like what happened to me was my fault.

I have come to tell you that no matter what... If this is happening or has happened to you, DON'T YOU EVER LET ANYONE MAKE YOU FEEL LIKE IT'S YOUR FAULT. No one ever has the right to ever violate you and please tell someone.

As I look back over my life, I often wonder what my life would've been like if I had just told one person. Me not dealing with my brokenness caused others to be broken such as my children and my family. I was bleeding on everybody and didn't even know it. At age 46, after going to drug and alcohol treatment, I realized that the little girl in me needed to be set free because I had been trapped long enough. My development had been arrested, and walls were put up. This deep, dark secret had affected every aspect of my life. No matter how much I tried to cover it up with nice clothes, jewelry, and makeup, the little girl and my pain would show up if you stepped on my toe hard enough.

Let me ask you a question, "Would you agree broken crayons still color?" I learned while being broken; I still had purpose and destiny. I only got derailed and off focus, but it wasn't the end. I learned I could forgive, heal, get back on track, and align with what God had for me to do. I also learned that what happened to me was not my fault, but it was every bit of my responsibility for how long I stayed in that place. Jeremiah 29:11 says, "For I know the plans I have for you, says the Lord. They are plans for good and not for evil, to give you a future and hope."

So, I decided to surrender and not look back, especially after I read that going back was like a dog returning to its vomit. Proverbs 26:11 states, As a dog returns to his vomit, so a fool repeats his foolishness. I was so desperate for change that I was determined to be teachable. I got in my Bible and did everything I could to become a doer of the word, not just a reader or hearer. I kept my eyes on Jesus, so I did not sink.

LET ME RE-INTRODUCE MYSELF

During my journey to healing and learning to live life in recovery, I learned that I was a leader. This could not have been made more apparent before going into a 28-day Drug and Alcohol Rehabilitation Program in Hoffman Estates. I would wake up early in the mornings before breakfast and go into the lounge, which was a common area. I would be the first one to write on the whiteboard. I read my Life Application Bible at night, which had practical applications as side notes to help you understand what the chapters were saying. So, whatever blessed me during my reading, I would share it by writing it on the whiteboard, and when the ladies would come into the lounge, it would also speak to where some of them were. Even those who would say they didn't believe in God. I would reword the scripture so no one would be offended since we had to respect each other's beliefs. This is where I learned how to give people the Word (Jesus) without them knowing that's what I was doing to keep from being offensive to those that didn't want to hear it. Looking back, I could say I was merging ministry and marketplace and didn't even know it.

Scriptures & Confessions

I MADE IT OUT

Below are scriptures and confessions of how I used them to get through the day. I had a lot of time on the side of addiction and very little time in this new walk and absence from drugs and alcohol. Early on in this journey, through the vessel God used, the late Apostle George Guilford, I learned how to make the scriptures personal by putting my name in them, seeing and speaking myself free, which I later came to know as affirmations and confessions.

I learned that death and life were in the power of my tongue (Proverbs 18:21). I also learned that words had power, so I had to speak what I wanted to see:

I AM AN OVERCOMER
I AM VICTORIOUS
I AM FREE
I AM NO LONGER A DRUG ADDICT
I AM DELIVERED.

I had to see myself that way daily, which was my confession. For I know the thoughts that you think towards me. Thoughts of good and not of evil, to give me a hope and an expected end (Jeremiah 29:11-13). This became one of my favorites because after hearing my life was not my own (I hadn't read that yet), I was sent into the earth from the spiritual realm with a specific assignment that only I could do. It made me eager to learn what my true purpose was. It was put to me like this, because I am very visual (there was something God needed done in the earth, so he looked around to see who he could send down to the earth to do it, and WHA-LA, I was chosen). He knew I would and could go through some things.

I have been redeemed, I've been bought with a price.
I Corinithians 6:20

I am a peculiar person called out of darkness into God's marvelous light.
I Peter 2:9

I had to remember that He was God, and He was a rewarder of those who diligently seek Him.
Hebrews 11:6

Greater is He that is in me than he that's in the world. I'm in the world, but not of it. I'M A KINGDOM CITIZEN NOW.
I John 4:4

I can't go back. I can't go back because it's like a dog returning to his vomit.
Proverbs 26:11

I must cast down all thoughts and imaginations that exalt themselves against my knowledge of God.
2 Corinthians 10:5-7

I used to tell myself, I can get through this because God has given me power and authority, which is the ability and the right to tread upon the serpents and scorpion and over all the power of the enemy and nothing shall hurt me.
Luke 10:19

I MADE IT OUT

God always hears me when I pray.
Psalm 35:17

God will never leave me nor forsake me.
Hebrews 13:5

If any man be in Christ, he is a new creation. Old things pass away and behold all things are new.
2 Corinithians 5:17

With Christ all things are possible.
Matthew 19:26

I can do all things with Christ who strengthens me.
Philippians 4:13

God you are strong when I am weak.

Lord, You are my Father, my Keeper, my Savior, my Redeemer, my Restorer, my Provider, my Peace, my Righteousness, my Healer, MY EVERYTHING.

Daily, I asked God to crawl with me, walk with me, run with me, and, when necessary, carry me.

BIOGRAPHY

Cheryl Edwards is an overcomer of drug addiction, alcoholism, and sexual abuse. She has taken her life experiences to mentor and coach others by using biblical strategies that have helped her regain her true identity in Christ. At 46, Cheryl was restored, renewed, and returned to her original state. After years of being processed, Cheryl accepted the calling to bring forth others who are currently struggling.

Cheryl's ministry is known as Restored Diamond. Her ministry is named after her daughter Ryan and her son Dorion. After leaving her children motherless for years, Cheryl was compelled to be a Comeback Kid for other broken families during her purification process. Cheryl believes that there is no such thing as a lost jewel. Restored Diamond Ministry believes that every addict, alcoholic, and abuse survivor can be brought back to their original identity by renouncing the stronghold and being cut out of bondage by seeing other's transparency, taking the strategies to apply them to everyday living, and hearing other's testimonies. Restored Diamond focuses on each person's value and purpose for which they were brought into the earth.

As I have cultivated what I see in others, I have had the opportunity to see my strengths as I help, build, and serve others with compassion.

I MADE IT OUT

YOUTUBE INTERVIEW

Use the space below to add your own scriptures or confessions and resources that you are using to journey through life's difficulties.

I MADE IT OUT

CHERYL EDWARDS

I MADE IT OUT

I MADE IT OUT

www.ingramcontent.com/pod-product-compliance
Lightning Source LLC
Chambersburg PA
CBHW070325100426
42743CB00011B/2566